Leaving My Homeland

A Refugee's Journey from
Yemen

Heather Hudak

 Crabtree Publishing Company
www.crabtreebooks.com

Crabtree Publishing Company
www.crabtreebooks.com

Author: Heather Hudak

Editors: Sarah Eason, Harriet McGregor, and Janine Deschenes

Proofreader and indexer: Wendy Scavuzzo

Editorial director: Kathy Middleton

Design: Jessica Moon

Cover design and additional artwork: Jessica Moon

Photo research: Rachel Blount

Production coordinator and Prepress technician: Ken Wright

Print coordinator: Margaret Amy Salter

Consultants: Hawa Sabriye and HaEun Kim

Produced for Crabtree Publishing Company by Calcium Creative.

Publisher's Note: The story presented in this book is a fictional account based on extensive research of real-life accounts by refugees, with the aim of reflecting the true experience of refugee children and their families.

Photo Credits:

t=Top, tr=Top Right, tl=Top Left

Inside: Shutterstock: Artskvortsova: p. 16l; Best-Backgrounds: p. 25; BigRoloImages: p. 7; Dmitry Chulov: pp. 10, 11; Claudiovidri: pp. 5b, 9b, 16tr; Daisyx: p. 12b; Dinosmichail: p. 8b; Love You: pp. 3, 26b; Macrovector: pp. 23t, 26t; Svetlana Maslova: p. 18b; MSSA: pp. 21tr, 28; Naeblys: p. 6; Palau: p. 13; Christine Ruddy: p. 23; Seita: p. 1; Globe Turner: p. 5tl; What's My Name: pp. 11b, 20t, 29t; Oleg Znamenskiy: pp. 8–9t; UNHCR: © UNHCR/Mohammed Al Hasani: p. 15; © UNHCR/Yahya Arhab: p. 21tl; © UNHCR/Mohamed Elfatih Elnaiem: pp. 18–19b, 26c; © UNHCR/Mohammed Hamoud: p. 14; © UNHCR/Oualid Khelifi: pp. 17b, 20b; © UNHCR/Hannah McNeish: p. 29; © UNHCR/Radonja Srdanovic: p. 24; Wikimeda Commons: Dnalyensid: p. 22; Pax Ahimsa Gethen: p. 27; Almigdad Mojalli/VOA: p. 4; Ibrahem Qasim: p. 12.

Cover: Shutterstock: Macrovector.

Library and Archives Canada Cataloguing in Publication

Hudak, Heather C., 1975-, author
    A refugee's journey from Yemen / Heather Hudak.

(Leaving my homeland)
Includes index.
Issued in print and electronic formats.
ISBN 978-0-7787-3677-6 (hardcover).--
ISBN 978-0-7787-3700-1 (softcover).--ISBN 978-1-4271-1974-2 (HTML)

    1. Refugees--Yemen (Republic)--Juvenile literature. 2. Refugees--Canada--Juvenile literature. 3. Refugee children--Yemen (Republic)--Juvenile literature. 4. Refugee children--Canada--Juvenile literature. 5. Refugees--Social conditions--Juvenile literature. 6. Yemen (Republic)--Social conditions--Juvenile literature. 7. Boat people--Yemen (Republic)--Juvenile literature. 8. Boat people--Canada--Juvenile literature. I. Title.

HV640.5.A6H83 2017   j305.9'0691409533   C2017-903587-8
    C2017-903588-6

Library of Congress Cataloging-in-Publication Data

CIP available at the Library of Congress

Crabtree Publishing Company
www.crabtreebooks.com   1-800-387-7650

Printed in Canada/092017/PB20170719

Published in Canada
Crabtree Publishing
616 Welland Ave.
St. Catharines, Ontario
L2M 5V6

Published in the United States
Crabtree Publishing
PMB 59051
350 Fifth Avenue, 59th Floor
New York, New York 10118

Published in the United Kingdom
Crabtree Publishing
Maritime House
Basin Road North, Hove
BN41 1WR

Published in Australia
Crabtree Publishing
3 Charles Street
Coburg North
VIC, 3058

What Is in This Book?

Leaving Yemen

A **civil war** began in Yemen in the spring of 2015. The war is between **rebel** fighters and the Yemeni government. The rebel fighters belonged to a minority, or small, group. They felt that the government did not treat them fairly. The rebels took power from the government and took control of many parts of Yemen. There is now fighting across the country.

Widespread fighting has left millions of Yemeni children without access to food, shelter, and health care.

UN Rights of the Child

Every child has rights. Rights are privileges and freedoms that are protected by law. **Refugees** have the right to special protection and help. The **United Nations (UN)** Convention on the Rights of the Child is a document that lists the rights that all children should have. Think about these rights as you read this book.

Thousands of people have been killed in the conflict. Millions have lost their homes. Some of these people remain in Yemen. They are **internally displaced persons (IDPs)**. Food and water are hard to find. There is no health care. People are dying of starvation and disease. Many buildings have been destroyed by bombs.

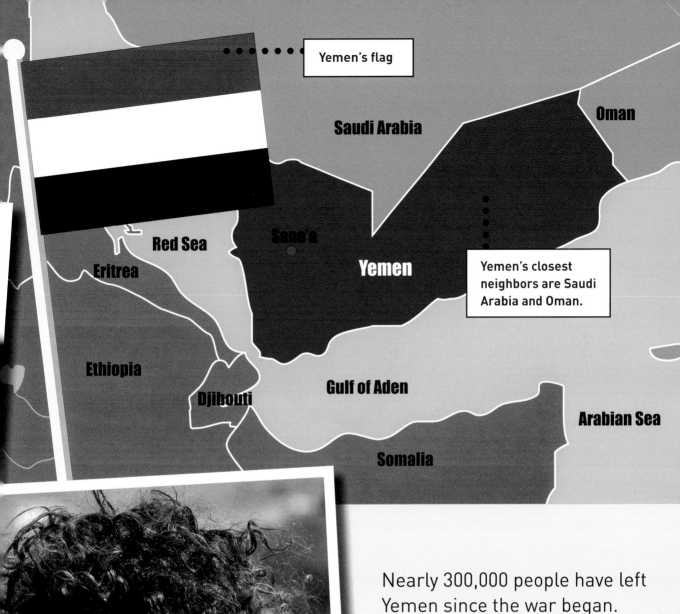

Yemen's flag

Oman

Saudi Arabia

Red Sea

Eritrea

Sana'a

Yemen

Yemen's closest
neighbors are Saudi
Arabia and Oman.

Ethiopia

Djibouti

Gulf of Aden

Arabian Sea

Somalia

Nearly 300,000 people have left
Yemen since the war began.
These people are refugees.
Refugees are people who left
their **homeland** because their
lives were in danger. They are
different from **immigrants**.
Immigrants chose to leave
to look for opportunities in
another country.

My Homeland, Yemen

Yemen is a small country in the **Middle East**. It is located between Saudi Arabia and Oman.

Much of Yemen is covered in desert. The **climate** is very hot and dry. About 75 percent of the people live in the countryside. Many live in the Sarat Mountains in the east of the country. The capital of Yemen, and the city with the largest population, is Sana'a. Almost all Yemeni people are Muslims. They follow a religion called Islam. Arabic is their main language.

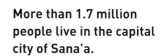

Sana'a

More than 1.7 million people live in the capital city of Sana'a.

Yemen is also known for its beautiful buildings, like these tall buildings in the capital city, Sana'a.

More than 92 percent of Yemenis are Arabs. The rest of the population is made up of Afro-Arabs, South Asians, and Europeans.

In ancient times, Yemen traded frankincense and myrrh, and many spices. Frankincense and myrrh are sweet smelling substances made from tree sap. Yemen was the first place where coffee was grown for commercial use, or to be bought and sold. Today, many parts of Yemen have been destroyed by bombs during the civil war. This has hurt its **industries**, making it one of the world's poorest countries.

Al Mukalla, a port city in southeastern Yemen, is the heart of its fishing industry.

Yemen's Story in Numbers

People have lived in Sana'a for more than

2,500 years.

Sahar's Story: Life Before War

My family lived in Sana'a. It was very beautiful. It had many tall brick buildings. There were many gardens between the buildings.

I was only eight when the civil war started. I had a very good life before the war. I lived with my parents, two younger brothers, and one younger sister. My uncle, aunt, and two small cousins also lived with us.

Al Saleh is the largest **mosque** in Sana'a. It has six minarets (tall, thin towers).

Before the war, many Yemeni children enjoyed going to school each day.

Yemen's Story in Numbers

Around 1,600 schools in Yemen have been closed due to the civil war. This has left an estimated

2 million

children out of school.

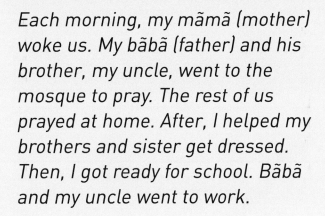

Each morning, my māmā (mother) woke us. My bābā (father) and his brother, my uncle, went to the mosque to pray. The rest of us prayed at home. After, I helped my brothers and sister get dressed. Then, I got ready for school. Bābā and my uncle went to work.

After work, Bābā often met his friends at the souk (market). Later, we all met to pray together.

After dinner, I helped Māmā tidy the house. Sometimes, I watched TV or played with my dolls before bed.

Parts of Sana'a have many souks, where locals shop for food, clothing, household items, jewelry, and more.

The Conflict in Yemen

For centuries, many countries have fought for power in Yemen. The British took control of southern Yemen in 1839. In the mid-1800s, the **Ottoman Empire** took control of northern Yemen. In 1904, they agreed to a border between their lands.

For many years, Yemen was split into two nations. There were many conflicts between North Yemen and South Yemen. Finally, they were united as the Republic of Yemen in 1990.

Government forces are fighting against Houthi rebels across Yemen.

This map shows where the country was split into North Yemen and South Yemen.

North Yemen

Sana'a

South Yemen

Aden

In the Hadramaut Valley and other parts of Yemen, security checkpoints are common.

Sana'a had been in North Yemen. It became the political capital of Yemen. Aden was a city in South Yemen. It became the **economic** capital of Yemen. Many people in South Yemen did not feel they were well **represented** in the government.

Yemen's economy was in poor shape. Many people could not find jobs. The government was corrupt, which means they did dishonest or illegal things to make money or gain power. By 2004, there was more fighting. A religious and political group called the Houthi rebelled. The Houthi wanted better treatment for people who follow a type of the Islam religion known as Zaidism.

By January 2015, fighting between Houthi rebels and the government increased. In February, the Houthi took over the government. By March, the fighting had turned into a civil war.

Sahar's Story: Living Amid the Fighting

I remember there was fighting in Yemen for a long time before the civil war started. People never seemed to be happy. It got much worse when the rebels took over our government. That is when the air raids started.

During the air raids, planes dropped bombs from the sky. It happened every day. I heard them flying overhead, sometimes for hours. There would be a whistling noise before a bomb fell. It was very scary.

Air strikes have destroyed a lot of Sana'a, killing many people and leaving others homeless.

I woke up one night to the sound of Māmā screaming. I ran out of my room to see if she was okay. I had only taken a few steps before I knew something was very wrong. Our home had been hit by a bomb. There were piles of rubble all around me.

I could still hear Māmā screaming, but I could not see her. There were clouds of dust everywhere. I found my sister under a pile of rocks. I screamed for Bābā. He came running. He was with one of my brothers. I held my brother while Bābā dug out my sister from under the rocks. I hugged my brother and sister close. My father went to find Māmā and my other brother.

My uncle and his family were safe. My aunt and cousins waited with me. My uncle went to help Bābā. When they found Māmā, she was injured. Her legs were caught under a pillar. My baby brother was crushed beneath the wreckage of our house. He could not breathe. Bābā tried hard to save him, but it was too late. We cried and cried.

Emergency workers came to help us. They took Māmā to the hospital. She stayed there for many weeks. She had three surgeries on her legs. But finally, we got some good news. She would be able to walk.

Nations Unite to Send Help

The UN helps keep peace between countries. It also provides help to people in need.

The UN department that helps refugees is called the United Nations High Commissioner for Refugees (UNHCR). Assistance provided by the UNHCR includes emergency food and housing.

More than 18 million people in Yemen struggle to find food. About 10 million of these people are in severe need. One in three children is **malnourished**.

Many displaced families have set up shelters at Dharwan. To be displaced means to be forced from your home. This shelter is just outside of Sana'a.

Yemen's Story in Numbers

Approximately
27.4 million
people live in Yemen.
Of them, about
18.8 million
people are in need of help.

One reason for this is because there is so much fighting that food suppliers cannot get shipments into the country.

More than 80 percent of the people living in Yemen urgently need help of some sort. But few are able to get the help they need. Fighting prevents supplies from getting to hospitals. Ambulances have no gas to run on. Hospitals cannot get the medicines they need. Many organizations around the world are trying to find ways to get help to people in Yemen.

The UNHCR provides blankets, mattresses, and other items to the hundreds of thousands of displaced people in Yemen.

Sahar's Story: We Flee from Sana'a

After our house was bombed, we had no place to live. We had to stay with some of our other family members. They did not have room for all of us. We had to split up between two or three houses. It was very hard to be apart.

My school had closed down, too. The bombs had destroyed it. I did not know where my friends were. I missed them and my brother terribly.

Approximately 1.4 million Yemeni children have been displaced.

Each day, there was more fighting. We could see smoke rising from buildings that had been bombed. Many parts of Sana'a had been destroyed. The city looked very different.

Bãbã said we needed to find safety away from Yemen. One night, he and Mãmã packed up our few belongings. They took us to a boat that was headed for Djibouti. To get there, we had to cross the long waterway that connects Yemen to Africa.

> Djibouti is a small country in northeastern Africa. It is approximately 270 miles (435 km) from Sana'a.

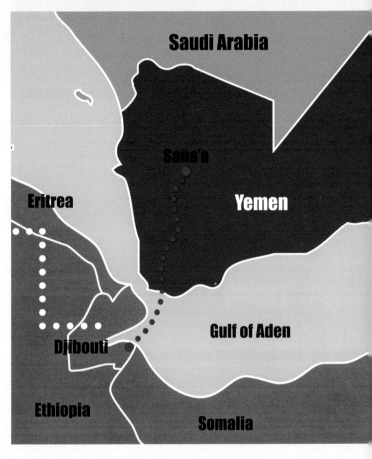

Saudi Arabia

Sana'a

Eritrea

Yemen

Gulf of Aden

Djibouti

Ethiopia

Somalia

Thousands of Yemenis have fled on boats like this to refugee camps in Djibouti.

I have heard people call the waterway the Gateway of Years because it is very dangerous. People sometimes die traveling through it. The water was very rough and made me feel sick. I held Mãmã's hand tightly and hoped we would be okay.

What Paths Do Refugees Take?

In 2016, Sudan accepted 1,688 Yemeni refugees.

Sudan

Most people who leave Yemen mainly flee to countries that are part of the Arab world. The Arab world consists of 22 countries in the Middle East. In these places, most people share the same language, religion, and **culture** as Yemenis.

1,454 Yemeni refugees left the country for Ethiopia in 2016.

Yemen's Story in Numbers

Many refugees from countries in Africa come to Yemen in hopes of traveling to Saudi Arabia to find work. They make the dangerous crossing from Djibouti to Yemen to escape conflict and poor living conditions in their homelands. But as Yemen becomes more dangerous, so do the journeys of refugees who travel through there. This list shows the number of refugees from other countries arriving in Yemen in 2015:

Ethiopia: 34,599   Other nations: 4

Somalia: 5,358

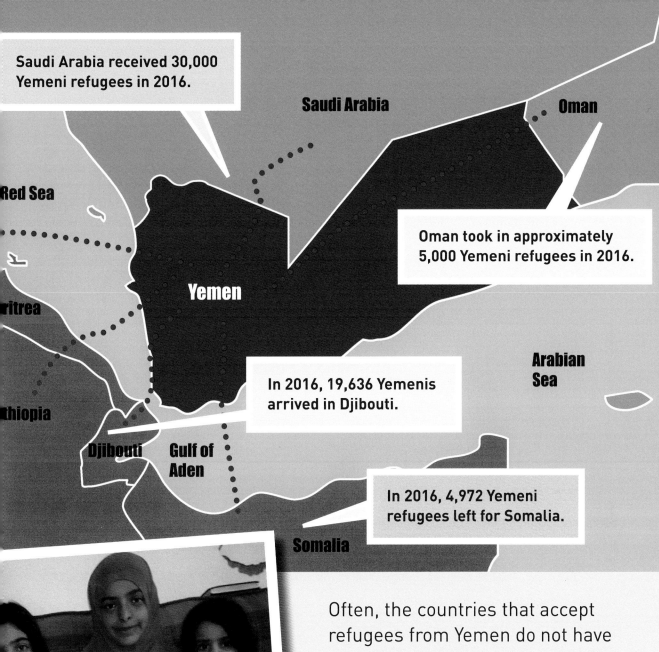

Saudi Arabia received 30,000 Yemeni refugees in 2016.

Saudi Arabia

Oman

Red Sea

Oman took in approximately 5,000 Yemeni refugees in 2016.

Yemen

Eritrea

Arabian Sea

Ethiopia

In 2016, 19,636 Yemenis arrived in Djibouti.

Djibouti   **Gulf of Aden**

In 2016, 4,972 Yemeni refugees left for Somalia.

Somalia

Often, the countries that accept refugees from Yemen do not have enough money or resources, such as shelter or health care, to care for all of the people who arrive. This means that the refugees do not receive the help they need.

A Yemeni refugee family starts their new life in Sudan.

Sahar's Story: My Life in Djibouti

I was so relieved when our boat finally reached Djibouti. Mãmã and Bãbã signed papers saying we were refugees. I would probably never go back to Yemen or see my friends again. That made me feel so sad.

We were sent to live at the Markazi refugee camp. I did not like it there. It was summertime, and the weather was very hot. I heard a rescue worker say it was 122 degrees Fahrenheit (50 °C) one day. The wind was strong and filled the air with sand and dust. Animals sometimes came into our tents, too.

Yemeni refugees have access to food and shelter at the Markazi camp in Obock, Djibouti.

Refugee shelters provide basic care and education for Yemeni children.

But I still felt safer at the camp than I did back home. At least there were no bombs or guns there. The people at the camp gave us each a thin sleeping mat. We had a small amount of food to eat, and clean water to drink.

The people at the camp let us make one three-minute phone call each day. Māmā called her brother and sister in Yemen. She wanted to make sure they were okay. They told her how bad the fighting was. She cried a lot when she talked to them.

It was not all bad at Markazi. My family made friends with three other Yemeni families. There was a small school. It was run by a charity and volunteer teachers. It did not have much, but at least I was learning new things.

Many of the Yemenis who came with us on our boat went back home. Others, like us, were hoping to be sent to another country to live.

Some Countries Welcome Refugees

Refugees are welcome in some countries around the world. These countries give refugees safe places to live. They help refugees build new lives.

Some countries will not accept Yemeni refugees. They think that because most Yemenis are Muslims they may be **terrorists**. The fear of Muslim people is called **Islamophobia**. It is an unfair **stereotype**. Refugees are not terrorists. They are people in search of a safe place to live.

These people are praying at the Lakemba Mosque. It is one of the largest mosques in Australia.

UN Rights of the Child

Every child has the right to live in freedom and dignity.

These people are protesting a travel ban that prevented people from Yemen and other countries from traveling to the United States in 2017.

Egypt has welcomed many Yemenis. Between 6,000 and 8,000 Yemenis live there now. Some were already there when the war broke out. Others fled there afterward.

Canada is known for welcoming people from around the world. From July 2015 to July 2016, more than 437,000 immigrants and refugees entered the country.

More than 1 million migrants and refugees went to Europe in 2015. Many come from Middle Eastern countries. They arrived in places such as Greece and Italy. They stayed in refugee camps until they could be sent to other European countries to live.

Sahar's Story: My New Home in Canada

The UNHCR helped Māmā and Bābā apply for **asylum**. We hoped to go to a country in Europe or North America. We waited many months to hear what would happen to us. Finally, we got the good news we would be going to Canada. Māmā was so happy that she cried. I had not seen her smile so big since before my baby brother died.

We got to ride in a big airplane. It was a long ride. I was scared we would fall from the sky. Volunteers met us when we got off the plane. They were very friendly and kind. They had warm parkas and boots for all of us. They even gave me a new doll.

This refugee Yemeni family was helped by the UNHCR to gain asylum in a new country.

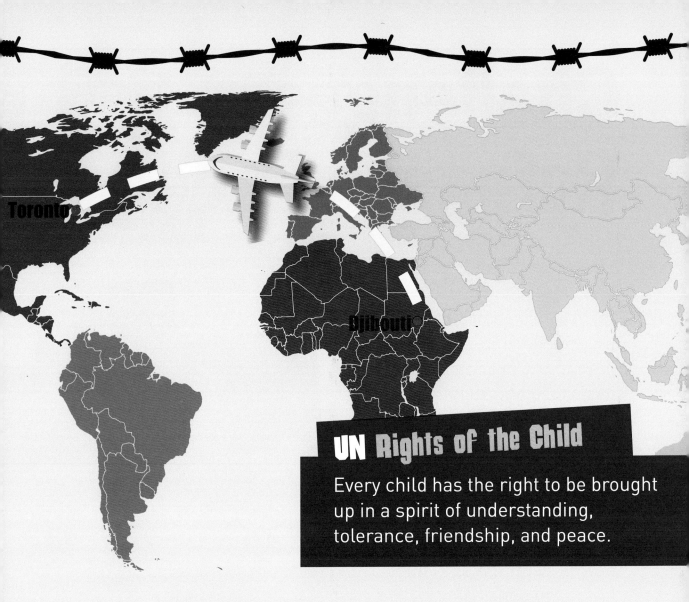

Toronto

Djibouti

UN Rights of the Child

Every child has the right to be brought up in a spirit of understanding, tolerance, friendship, and peace.

It was the middle of winter when we arrived in Toronto. I had never been so cold. Canada was very different from Yemen. We were given a small apartment to stay in. It was in a suburb of Toronto. We were also given some money to buy food and clothing. Bãbã got a job working in a warehouse. Mãmã is taking English classes at a community college.

I go to school with hundreds of other kids. At first, it was hard. I could not speak much English. But I soon made friends with some of the other girls. I miss my friends and family in Yemen. I hope to return one day when the fighting is over. People in Canada have been very kind to us. My family is finally safe and happy.

Challenges Refugees Face

Life as a refugee is not easy. Most refugees have fled terrible living conditions in their homelands. Often, they have to live in camps with only basic food and supplies. They wait a long time to find a **host country** that will accept them.

When they arrive in the host country, they face many new challenges. Most refugees have very little money and few belongings. They have to rebuild their entire lives.

Families that were separated in Yemen can live together in their host countries.

UN Rights of the Child

You have the right to choose your own religion and beliefs.

Taking part in events, such as this pro-refugee demonstration in San Francisco, is one way to help refugees feel at home in their new countries.

Often, refugees do not speak the language of their host country. This makes it difficult for them to do even simple tasks. Taking a bus or buying groceries can be hard to do. Many refugees are well educated, and had very good jobs in their homelands. But it can be difficult for them to find jobs in their host countries if they do not speak the local language. Filling out forms, such as job and health care applications, is a challenge. Children may find it hard to do schoolwork or make friends if they cannot speak the language.

Most refugees live in a host country that has a very different culture than their homeland. It can be hard to adjust to different ways of life. Refugees may be used to dressing or eating differently than the people in their host country. It can be difficult to practice their culture and traditions in their host country.

You Can Help!

There are many things you can do to help refugees from places such as Yemen. Learning about another culture and putting yourself in a newcomer's position is a good place to start.

 Read books, watch movies, or surf the Internet to learn about Yemeni culture and Islam. Share what you have learned with your friends.

 Offer to show new students around your school and neighborhood. Introduce them to your friends and family.

 Find out about Yemeni celebrations and holidays. Attend events in honor of them.

 Learn a few words in Arabic, such as "ahlan wa sahlan" (hello) and "motashakr awi" (many thanks).

 Volunteer with a local organization that helps refugees. Together with your family, you can also learn about and support international organizations that help refugees.

AID

Yemeni refugees, such as this boy in a tented camp in Djibouti, have likely known great suffering before arriving in their new country.

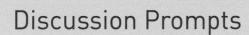

Discussion Prompts

1. Explain the difference between a refugee, an immigrant, and an IDP.
2. Explain why a person might become a refugee.
3. How can you help newcomers feel welcome in their new home?

Glossary

asylum Protection given to refugees by a country

civil war A war between groups of people in the same country

climate The typical weather conditions of an area

culture The shared beliefs, values, customs, traditions, arts, and ways of life of a particular group of people

economic The system of how money is made and used in a country

homeland The country where someone was born or grew up

host country A country that offers to give refugees a home

immigrants People who leave one country to live in another

industries Making products or processing materials

internally displaced persons (IDPs) People who are forced from their homes during a conflict, but remain in their country

Islamophobia A fear or dislike of Muslims

malnourished When someone becomes sick because they do not have enough to eat

Middle East Countries in southwestern Asia and northern Africa that stretch from Libya to Afghanistan

mosque Muslim place of worship

Ottoman Empire A Turkish Empire that ruled in southeastern Europe, western Asia, and northern Africa from the 1300s to the early 1900s

rebel A person who fights against the government of a country

refugees People who flee from their own country to another due to unsafe conditions

represented Officially spoken for by someone else

stereotype An idea held about someone or something that is usually untrue

terrorists People who use violence or intimidation to achieve their political goals

United Nations (UN) An international organization that promotes peace between countries and helps refugees

Learning More

Books

Kuntz, Doug. *Lost and Found Cat: The True Story of Kunkush's Incredible Journey.* Crown Books for Young Readers, 2017.

Righton, Nathalie. *Children Just Like You and Other Refugee Stories.* Lemniscaat USA, 2012.

Robinson, Anthony, and Annemarie Young. *Mohammed's Journey (A Refugee Diary).* Francis Lincoln Children's Books, 2011.

Ruurs, Margriet. *Stepping Stones: A Refugee Family's Journey.* Orca Book Publishers, 2016.

Websites

www.ducksters.com/geography/country.php?country=Yemen
Learn interesting facts about Yemen's location, people, and economy.

www.savethechildren.org/site/c.8rKLIXMGIpI4E/b.6153153/k.BDE3/ Yemen.htm?msource=weolpyemv013
Read all about the work Save the Children is doing to help children in Yemen.

stories.unhcr.org/bushras-story-yemen-p3975.html
Watch a short movie about Bushra, a refugee girl from Yemen.

www.unrefugees.org/what-is-a-refugee
Learn more about what it means to be a refugee and an IDP.

Index

About the Author

Heather C. Hudak has written hundreds of books for children and edited thousands more. She loves traveling the world, learning about new cultures, and spending time with her husband and many pets.